CONTENTS

C000150264

AUTHOR
Patrick Martin

EDITOR
Jason Monaghan

IMAGE EDITOR
Lisa Burton

Front Cover:
Dunsinane on the rocks outside St Sampsons.
F.W. Guerin, 1904.

The author has made every effort to ensure
the accuracy of the information within this
book was correct at the time of publication.

All maps shown are for general illustrative
location purposes only and are not intended
to aid in locating wreck sites. Many of
the wreck sites described in this book are
protected by law.

SHIPS IN TROUBLE

Vessels have been sailing through the waters of Guernsey for over 4,000 years. Flint tools and pottery were brought here from France in simple boats as long ago as 2,500BC. From as early as 120BC the island was a waypoint on the trade route bringing Roman wine to the Celtic tribes of Britain and northern Gaul. Viking seamen gave the islands their modern names, and named their most prominent islets and headlands as seamarks. St Peter Port is the best natural harbour in the Channel Islands, attracting merchants and warships in centuries past and today welcoming tourists and yachtsmen. Guernsey offers plentiful opportunities for serious yachtsmen, beautiful spots for family boating excursions, and exciting dive sites. In the right weather, and with an experienced skipper, it is a magical region.

Contest in high seas

SHIPS IN TROUBLE

Where there is a lot of shipping there is often a high number of shipwrecks and Guernsey has seen its share over the centuries. The huge tidal range exceeds ten metres, there are many dangerous reefs, and the currents are strong as the tides sweep in and out of the Bay of St Malo.

Even in good conditions things can go wrong at sea, but when a storm of great force comes in, a ship's position is miscalculated, the sails are down or the engines can't cope, risk increases. The sea is rough, the tide is flowing fast and perhaps visibility is poor. Especially in the past, the chance of tragedy was increased when navigation aids were crude, lifeboats insufficient and most sailors could not swim.

Guernsey is a triangular shape, with 100-metre cliffs along the south coast, long flat beaches and rocky headlands on the west, and the excellent sheltered harbour of St Peter Port on the east coast. 10,000 years ago the islands formed part of the European continent, but as sea levels rose after the end of the Ice Age, the higher areas were left as separate islands off the coast of Normandy. Raised beaches exist throughout the islands showing where former changes in sea levels created wave-cut platforms and

small cliffs. The sea is relatively shallow, and hundreds of rocks and reefs appear at low tide up to two miles from shore. To avoid accidents off Guernsey's west coast, in 1971 the shipping lanes were moved further out.

Although a map of Guernsey waters shows shipwrecks almost everywhere, a high concentration is close to the harbour (where most shipping was) and on two especially treacherous reefs: the Hanois off the south-west tip of Guernsey and the Casquets to the west of Alderney. The latter lie on the main sea route to England, so ships have to alter course to negotiate this dangerous series of 'helmets', and in fog or stormy weather there is little room for error. Lighthouses were eventually built to reduce the toll of shipping taken by these reefs.

Well over 800 shipwrecks are known from historic periods in these waters, and many more ancient ones have undoubtedly been forgotten. The selection chosen for this book covers a range of incidents in order to reveal the scale and variety of wrecks that have occurred. It is to some extent also a snapshot of Guernsey's maritime history.

Photographs and illustrations are taken in the most part from the collections of Guernsey Museums & Galleries unless otherwise indicated.

FORT GREY
SHIPWRECK MUSEUM

A Shipwreck Museum was opened in 1975 at Fort Grey in Rocquaine Bay. The Fort is on a small islet about 50 metres off the beach, reached by a causeway. It is a 'Martello Tower' built in 1804 during the Napoleonic Wars as part of the defences proposed by the Governor Sir John Doyle. It replaced the 15th century Château de Rocquaine which formerly stood on the same spot. Before the Fort was turned into a museum, the only way in was over the wall by ladder or rope. The men who built the Hanois lighthouse off Pleinmont point in 1862 were housed in the Fort during the work. German occupying forces also used it between 1940 and 1945, and they made the window on the south side of the tower. The Shipwreck Museum now houses a collection of objects from west coast wrecks, maps and charts, rescue equipment and models. It is an iconic landmark known to locals as 'The Cup and Saucer'.

VisitGuernsey

ROMAN SHIPWRECKS

CIRCA 280-286

The ship was destroyed by fire and sank in shallow water between the pierheads of St Peter Port harbour.

ST PETER PORT HARBOUR

A third-century Roman ship was discovered between the pierheads of St Peter Port harbour in 1982 and raised by archaeologists between 1984 and 1986. Popularly known as 'Asterix', it was a merchant ship measuring about 25m long and 6m wide built in a Romano-Celtic style. It is the largest and most intact sea-going vessel of its antiquity found outside the Mediterranean, and of great international maritime significance. The ship was carvel-built (with smooth edge-to-edge planking) using oak, and she had a single sail (possibly made of leather) placed about one third of the way back from the bow. The shipwrights used iron nails up to 750mm long to fasten the planking to the huge frame timbers. She was probably a coaster, carrying general cargoes from port to port. With a flat bottom, she could easily beach when bad weather was approaching, or enter shallow estuaries or harbours. This made her a useful design for the dangerous waters of the region where there were few proper

Penny Dorey

harbours. Ships like this may have been used as long ago as 56BC when Julius Caesar describes fighting Gauls sailing similar vessels.

Local diver Richard Keen spotted the exposed timbers sticking out of the sea-bed sediments on Christmas Day 1982, the only day in the year when divers were allowed to dive in the harbour mouth. Propeller wash from big new passenger ferries had scoured away the seabed and was starting to break up the ship. Dr Margaret Rule, who raised the Mary Rose, was called in to lead the rescue which became known as 'Operation Asterix'.

ROMAN SHIPWRECKS

FIND OUT MORE

Dr Margaret Rule and her assistant Dr Jason Monaghan wrote the definitive book on the subject *'A Gallo-Roman Trading Vessel from Guernsey'*. Objects from the ship are on show in Castle Cornet and the ship's main timbers were put on view close to Fort Grey in 2015.

Archaeologists worked quickly to record and excavate the site, and to raise the timbers, before the planned dredging of the harbour started. Some timbers were 7m long, weighing as much as half a tonne. After being examined, cleaned and recorded ashore, they were sent to the Mary Rose Trust in Portsmouth to be preserved using polyethylene glycol wax (PEG) and freeze-drying.

Evidence shows that the ship was destroyed by fire and sank in shallow water. On board were blocks of pine tar which melted in the fire and flowed around her aft hold. This solidified in the water and effectively preserved the stern of the ship, and much of what was carried there. Coins indicate that the ship sank between AD 280 and 286. Pieces of pottery on board came from Algeria, Spain, Britain and Gaul (France), suggesting the ship worked the Atlantic trade routes and that Guernsey was an entrepôt for this trade in Roman times.

'Asterix' is not our only Roman ship, however. A second ship wrecked just outside the harbour was carrying fish-sauce in distinctive Spanish amphorae of the later 1st to mid-2nd century AD. Another three to five wreck sites are suspected in the Little Russel channel, shown by finds of millstones, pottery and Spanish and Gallic wine amphorae. Guernsey in fact has the highest concentration of Roman shipwreck sites in British waters.

Guernsey Press

MEDIEVAL HARBOUR WRECKS

CIRCA 1300-1450

The eight ships were found 600m from the mouth of the old medieval harbour.

ST PETER PORT HARBOUR

Between 1985 and 2003 the remains of up to 8 medieval trading ships were discovered in a small area near Castle Cornet and the pierheads of St Peter Port harbour. Just as with the Roman ship, the sand and silt that had helped to preserve them for so long was being churned up by propeller wash from ferries and harbour dredging.

In the 14th century the wreck site would have been 600m from the mouth of the old medieval harbour. The site was flanked by two rocky reefs: the White Rock and the rocks on which Castle Cornet stands. It is thought that larger ships which could enter the old harbour only at high tide may have anchored here to unload their cargoes onto smaller boats. Any ship caught in a storm in the 'inner roads' could have faced disaster.

Guernsey's position assured her a significant place in north-south trade during the middle ages. Ships frequently visited the island, but not much is recorded about comings and goings or about their cargoes. We know from the records of harbour dues that 487 ships visited in the year 1330 alone.

Guernsey traded with Brittany and Normandy, and was also an important entrepôt for the wine trade between south-west France and England. Essential goods were imported: wood, coal, bricks, wheat, glass and metal. A triangular trade was also developing which would carry stores to the Newfoundland fisheries, collect fish to ship to the Mediterranean, then wine and fruit to bring back to Guernsey and England.

When King John lost Normandy to the French in 1204, Guernsey's strategic importance grew. A period of military skirmishes followed between the French and the English. This could perhaps explain the unusual concentration of wrecks all from about the same time. Divers have photographed and made

plans of the ships as they have been revealed, but only one was briefly raised and moved to a safer location. The rest remain on the seabed and some have broken up.

The ships were all clinker-built (with hull-planks overlapping) in the Nordic tradition which dominated western European shipbuilding until the carvel style (with smooth edge-to-edge planking) came into vogue in the 16th century. The age of the wrecks has been established by using dendrochronological testing to examine the growth-rings of timbers. One of the ships was a particularly large medieval 'Great Ship' over 25m long and 7m wide. The others are also fairly large, some more than 20m long. The oak hulls were fastened with wooden pegs, and the joints were caulked with sphagnum moss.

When harbours are dredged, or during construction work, wrecked ships are often found. The probability is that other medieval wrecks are still to be found in and around St Peter Port harbour.

Brian Byron

13

LA VIERGE DE BON PORT

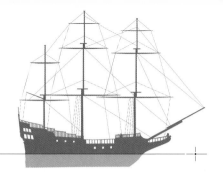

JULY 9, 1666

Sunk by an English Frigate somewhere off the west coast of Guernsey.

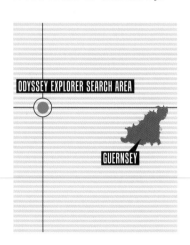

ODYSSEY EXPLORER SEARCH AREA

GUERNSEY

During 2009 a large yellow ship full of high-tech diving and searching equipment was seen moving in zig-zags off the west coast of Guernsey. Its movements could be followed on any computer by opening the Digimap marine service of AIS (automatic identification system). She was *Odyssey Explorer*, belonging to Odyssey Marine Exploration, a company that searches the oceans for wrecks that might contain great treasure. Rumour had it that she was looking for *La Vierge de Bon Port*.

A huge amount of treasure was on board *La Vierge* when she sank in 1666, but the exact location has been a mystery. She was an East Indiaman, a very large armed vessel for trading and exploration. With the approval of Louis XIV the French East India Company bought her in St Malo in 1664 with a very special purpose in mind: to explore Madagascar and determine its potential as a colony. It would be important for further investment that the first expedition of

four ships brought back interesting and valuable samples of treasures.

La Vierge de Bon Port weighed 300 tons and carried 22 guns. Four ships met in Brest and set off on 7 March 1665, arriving in Madagascar five months later. After six months exploring, loading up the ships as they went, they set off back for France in February 1666. The value of the cargo was put at an incredible £1,500,000, but this was probably an underestimate as precious stones and ambergris (originating from the intestine of the sperm whale) alone came to about half a million pounds.

On 8 July 1666 *La Vierge de Bon Port* entered the English Channel heading for Le Havre, intending to unload close to Paris. The ship was dressed up magnificently for a triumphant return. The captain, Trouchet, was completely unaware that France had declared war on England on 9 January. If they had known this he would have kept well off Guernsey. Indeed when the crew spotted land they wrongly thought Guernsey was the French coast near Cherbourg.

The French ship was approached on 9 July by *Orange Tree*, an English frigate out of St Peter Port, a corsair or privateering vessel under the command of Christopher Gunman. His ship opened fire on the French, perhaps only three miles west of the Hanois reef. Fighting went on for five hours until the masts of *La Vierge* were brought down, she was on fire and holed in four places at the waterline. The surgeon could not get around to all the wounded.

La Vierge was boarded and looted. The French called out for surrender, but because of a misunderstanding the fighting continued. The water pumps could not cope, so when *La Vierge* started to sink she went down quickly and many men were trapped below decks. Some were rescued, taken to St Peter Port and later to prison in the Isle of Wight. Captain Trouchet died there before he could explain the reasons for the disaster.

It is thought that *La Vierge de Bon Port* is still holding one of the greatest treasures of any shipwreck, but the mystery lies waiting to be solved.

A.M. Malet, circa 1690

HMS SPRIGHTLY

DECEMBER 23, 1777

Capsized south east of the Hanois reef, off the south west tip of Guernsey.

HANOIS REEF

HMS Sprightly was built at the Royal Dockyard at Dover, and launched on 16 August 1777. She put to sea under Lieutenant Hills, and capsized off Guernsey four months later. The fate of none of the 17 men thought to have been on board is known.

Sprightly was one of about 20 Royal Navy cutters which were operating during the late 18th century. A cutter was a fast ship with 10 to 12 guns, used for despatch duties, scouting, chasing pirate ships, and also for the suppression of smuggling when inshore. They were prone to capsizing because of over-canvassing.

In 1973 a professional Belgian diver, Robert Stenuit, was exploring south-east of the Hanois with his team including local diver Richard Keen. At the site, the water is not deep but the currents are strong and it was difficult to work in the rock crevasses and along ledges. The divers found Royal Navy Ordnance with broad arrow markings, two dozen gold guineas bearing the head of George III, and a fine pistol by Clarkson of London. Examination of naval records helped to identify the wreck.

Stenuit says that a marine archaeologist, like a detective, looks for evidence which he can later examine to establish the identity of a wreck. An amazing variety of material was found in the debris zone. Eventually each piece was traced by date and type to its original foundry in England. A drawing exists of *Sprightly's* 'twin brother', *Hawk*, which was built at the same yard, in the same year, following identical design plans.

Robert Sténuit

FIND OUT MORE

In the Shipwreck Museum at Fort Grey, the Sprightly display case contains a candlestick and sealing wax, razors, spoons, some sail canvas, a small cannon, wine glasses, buckles, and a stoneware jar.

HMS BOREAS

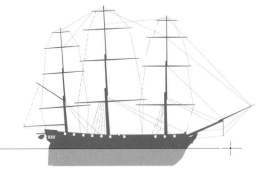

NOVEMBER 28, 1807

Struck the Hanois reef off the south west tip of Guernsey in a gale and sank.

CUTTER IN TOW

HIT ROCK AT HANOIS REEF

In 1805 work started building a fine new frigate for the Royal Navy. Weighing 533 tons, and carrying 195 officers and men, she was armed with a range of guns including 18-pound carronades with great power at close quarters. The ship was named *HMS Boreas* and launched at Great Yarmouth on 19 April 1806.

The threat of a French invasion had eased at this time, and the duty of British warships based in Guernsey was more relaxed. *Boreas* captured the French schooner *Victoire* out of Morlaix, which had taken an American brig the day before.

On 28 November 1807, as *Boreas* was returning to Guernsey during a gathering storm, she was alerted to some cutter pilots who were in trouble off Lihou Island on the west coast of Guernsey. *Boreas* immediately sailed along the south coast to Pleinmont, safely avoiding the notorious Hanois reef as she turned north across Rocquaine Bay. She found the pilots and took them on board, and took their cutter in

tow. It was cloudy and the breeze was now a hard north-easterly.

What happened next is uncertain, but the intention was to set course for St Peter Port harbour. Perhaps the course setting was inexact, or else the gale drove *Boreas* off her line, but the ship struck a rock. She was in the middle of the Hanois reef with dozens of rocky outcrops and fast-flowing channels all around, and it had become dark as well as stormy.

The commander, Captain Robert Scott, ordered more sail in order to drive his ship forward and off the rock. However, within 30 metres *Boreas* was on another rock, holed below the water-line and stuck fast. Even if the Navy's local knowledge here was wanting, the pilots would certainly have known the bay in detail, yet surprisingly they do not seem to have helped. In fact, it is reported that they returned to their cutter, cut the rope, and disappeared!

FIND OUT MORE

In the Shipwreck Museum at Fort Grey, the *Boreas* case has a display of musket balls, brass and copper nails, a bronze clamp, and a pocket knife.

Throughout the night there were examples of great bravery mixed with disgraceful cases of unwillingness to help. *Boreas* fired her guns and showed lights, but it was a stormy night and people ashore either remained unaware or did not want to risk going to help. Water was pumped out, and the masts were cut to try to stabilise the ship, but neither was ultimately effective.

Some men were ordered ashore in small boats, but instead of returning to the ship for more men, they escaped into the night. Such desertion resulted in far fewer men surviving overall. Local fishermen were reluctant to put to sea, either because of the weather or because it wasn't clear if the ship was French or English.

By daylight *Boreas* had disappeared under the waves, apart from some of the rigging. Loss of a ship meant of course that there would be a court martial. The number of survivors was put at 77,

but the Captain and most of the ship's complement were lost. It was never established exactly how many drowned, but estimates vary between 53 and 103. The Court Martial cleared all officers and crew of blame, but the deserters would be hanged if caught.

One of Guernsey's most successful and respected divers, Richard Keen, made some exploratory dives on the Hanois in 1969, having first done some research and estimates of the location of the wreck. In an area such as this, rock is broken up and eroded very quickly because of the powerful destructive force of the waves and currents. Yet what he found on shallow ledges was really surprising: a number of artefacts from *Boreas* had survived.

One of these artefacts was a cannon which would be very appropriate for the new Shipwreck Museum which was opening at Fort Grey. Because of difficulties with access, it was decided

to request help from the Navy with one of their helicopters. A Wessex carried the cannon across the bay to the Fort, and the *Boreas* cannon was placed on a carriage facing the reef where the ship had met her fate. The loss of *Boreas* was just one of a sad succession of Hanois wrecks which finally resulted in a lighthouse being constructed there.

ONEIDA

DECEMBER 19, 1849

Struck rocks off the north-west of Guernsey before being driven in to Perelle Bay.

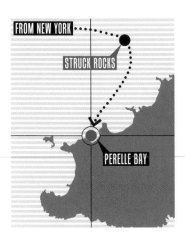

In the middle of the night of 19-20 December 1849 an American packet ship en route from New York to Le Havre was sailing up the Channel with 28 crew and 22 passengers on board. *Oneida* weighed 791 tons, and was under the control of Captain Willard.

She first struck rocks about two miles off the north-west coast of Guernsey, and was then driven onto rocks at the south end of Perelle Bay. The vessel's back broke, her rudder was unshipped and the main mast was sprung. The crew cut the mast away, and it drifted out to sea with its sails and rigging. Waves were breaking violently over the ship, and when the boats were lowered they were dashed to pieces. The long boat could not even be launched, so passengers and crew remained on the ship.

At daybreak around 5am the stricken ship could be seen from shore, and some small boats put out, but they had great difficulty approaching in the breaking surf. Finally, as the boats approached under the bows, the crew lowered some passengers by sling from the bowsprit. When Lloyd's agent, Henry Tupper, arrived he advised the captain to keep all hands on board, because in an hour or two when the tide had fallen they could land in safety.

All passengers, crew, and personal effects were safely brought ashore. Those rescued were all taken to nearby houses and later into St Peter Port. Among the passengers were a number of poor German emigrants who had not found work in America and were travelling home in steerage. Also on board was a French artist, Dr Edouart, who had been cutting silhouettes of famous people

Peter Le Lievre

in America, and he was travelling with a valuable collection of his work, much of which was saved.

The ship was a total wreck. The value of *Oneida* and her 1000 tons of cargo was put at £20,000. The US consul, Mr Le Marchant, directed the work of unloading the cargo with men, carts and horses. The rate was 12 shillings and 6 pence (62.5p) a bale to the high water mark. As many as 400 people worked to unload most of the cargo of cotton, stone and tallow, which was taken in three local brigs to Le Havre. The 100 tons of stone in ballast broke away her bottom as the tide rose, and was salvaged and stored at the depot in the Bouet in town. The mast, sails and rigging were also picked up, but total salvage costs came to £3000. The Star newspaper carried a notice on 15 January 1850 for an auction to take place on 17 January of timber from the wreck of *Oneida*; less than £200 was raised.

Letters in the newpapers referred to the pilfering and looting that occurred, and also the fact that some people expected financial reward for helping wrecks. The Royal Court in St Peter Port however awarded £10 to four Guernseymen for their courage in rescuing five of the sailors.

Inquiry into the wrecking established that the captain had mistaken the Casquets lighthouse near Alderney for a light on the English coast. It was clear again that a light was needed on the north or west of Guernsey.

BOSTONIAN

JANUARY 2, 1861

Struck the Hanois reef off the south western tip of Guernsey.

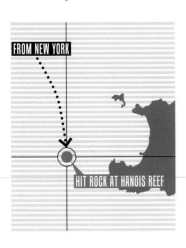

FROM NEW YORK

HIT ROCK AT HANOIS REEF

A serious error in navigation resulted in the large cargo vessel *Bostonian* ending up on rocks on the west coast of Guernsey. A few hours before, she had in turn rescued the crew of another ship in trouble.

Bostonian, under Captain Charles Brookman, entered the Channel on New Year's Day 1861 after crossing the Atlantic. She had been built in 1855, weighed 1017 tons, and was valued at £10,000. She was carrying flour, wheat, cheese and general cargo from New York to London. Her cargo was valued at £30,000.

The brig *Aire* under Captain Slingsby had meanwhile got into difficulties going down the Channel while on a passage from London to Malta with 300 tons of government stores. Heavy seas were sweeping her decks and one man had been swept overboard. The American master of *Bostonian* spotted *Aire* in distress and he took the crew on board. Slingsby had thought he was 20 miles

south of the Eddystone lighthouse, but the compass reading was wrong as it had been damaged by seawater.

The mid-winter weather was foul and the Met Office recorded a "strong gale with violent gusts from the SSW". Records show that a deep depression went almost over the top of Guernsey that day. Visibility had been very poor for most of *Bostonian's* voyage, and she had made only three observations of the sun on the whole passage. On the night of 1-2 January it was Captain Brookman's turn to make a mistake when he identified the Eddystone lighthouse incorrectly.

Continuing up the Channel, Brookman saw the Casquets light off Alderney but mistook it for Start Point in Devon. He turned to head southeast, but was in fact getting closer to Guernsey in the middle of a stormy night. At 4am on 2 January *Bostonian* struck a rock, but got off. At 5.30am she was driven onto a reef, which at first Brookman thought was Les Grunes, but as The Star newspaper reported on 3 January it was the Hanois.

The wind veered northwest and the tide was flowing fast in the same direction. Pilots from Rocquaine were able to rescue 18 sailors who were clinging to the rigging, but the master, six of his crew, and two of *Aire's* crew, were lost. The captain had run aft to secure a life-buoy but was swept overboard and lost. The vessel was a total loss.

The Star observed:
"Had the lighthouse now in course of erection been finished, this accident would not have occurred. Surely this is another warning to our authorities to see to this very important matter".
By the following year the Hanois lighthouse was operating.

'Clipper ship *Bostonian* off Hong Kong.' Copyright 2015 by The Kelton Foundation

YOROUBA

APRIL 13, 1888

Struck the Gibou rocks off Lihou Island, and sank just to the north of this spot.

HIT GIBOU ROCKS

LIHOU ISLAND

FROM MARSEILLES

The very first steam vessel to visit Guernsey had been *Medina*, a paddle steamer, in 1823. Previously, mail and passengers travelled on sailing packets. *Yorouba* was a brigantine-rigged steamer, a combination of sail and screw that was common in the late 19th century. If the engines failed, or were shut down to save coal, such a ship could still sail.

Yorouba had been built in Barrow, and was later bought by Messageries Maritimes, the French shipping company. She weighed 1246 tons, and set out from Marseilles with a cargo of wool, cotton, oil and iron ore bound for Le Havre and London. On board were her captain Henri Charvau, 35 crew and 15 passengers.

The weather was fine passing Gibraltar and across Biscay, but fog in the Channel prevented any observations for two days. It is reported that *Yorouba's* crew sighted the Casquets light, but they may have misidentified it, for instead of keeping north of the light she continued on slowly until she thumped heavily into the Gibou rocks off Lihou Island, south of her proper course. It was 0035 hours on 13 April 1888.

The Star newspaper reported that all crew and passengers got into four boats in the dark, along with the ship's papers and chronometers. *Yorouba* slid off the rocks and settled in about 12 fathoms (22m) of water.

With the sea very calm, the boats remained around the wreck. Everyone had been rescued. At daylight the crew rowed ashore to a house at the Crocq where plentiful refreshments were provided. Later everyone was taken to St Peter Port where the French Consul further provided for all of them.

The vessel was not insured, but at least the £10,000 cargo was. The insurers asked for the cargo to be saved, but that was an almost impossible task because even at low tide *Yorouba* was covered with water, and only her masts were visible.

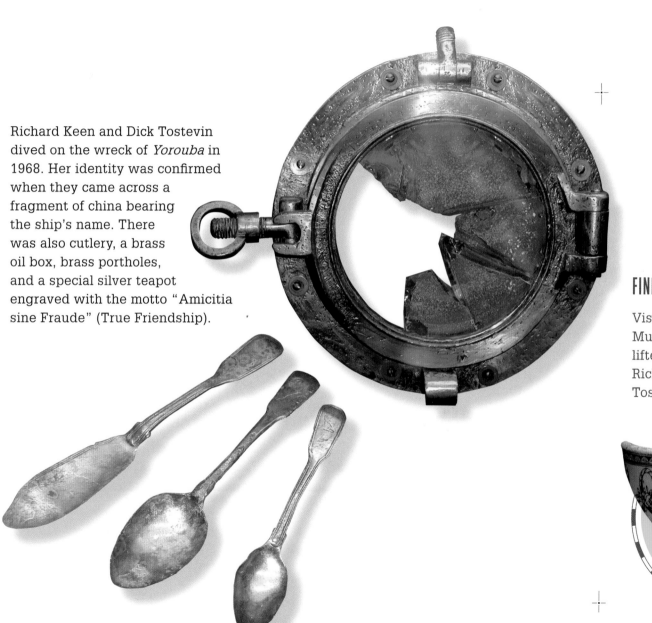

Richard Keen and Dick Tostevin dived on the wreck of *Yorouba* in 1968. Her identity was confirmed when they came across a fragment of china bearing the ship's name. There was also cutlery, a brass oil box, brass portholes, and a special silver teapot engraved with the motto "Amicitia sine Fraude" (True Friendship).

FIND OUT MORE

Visit Fort Grey Shipwreck Museum to see objects lifted from the wreck by Richard Keen and Dick Tostevin in 1968.

STELLA

MARCH 30, 1899

Struck the Casquets reef, 5 miles west of Alderney, and sank just to the south of this spot

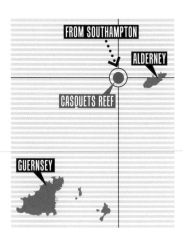

Stella was built in Glasgow in 1890 as the third in the London and South Western Railway Company fleet of fast cross-channel passenger steamers. She was powerful for her size, and with three-bladed twin screws she was capable of almost 20 knots. This fine ship sank in 1899, in the most tragic disaster in local seas since the *Boreas*. She later became known as 'The Titanic of the Channel Islands'.

The luxury of her interiors was unequalled in Channel shipping. There were electric lights, very comfortable ladies' and gentlemen's saloons, first and second class cabins, carved oak panels, fine glassware, and silver cutlery. All of this comfort tended to lull passengers into a sense of safety which was completely misplaced. While ships had advanced tremendously in speed and luxury, their navigational systems were hopelessly outdated. With no radio, no radar, no echo-sounder, navigation relied on casting the lead, observing markers, and dead reckoning.

On 30 March 1899, the crossing from Southampton began in a spirit of great euphoria. People were going to the islands for Easter, and the day-time trip was the first of a new season. William Reeks, the captain, had 25 years experience at sea and 8 years as master, and he was confident that this would be a fast run which would enhance his reputation. In fact he was quoted as saying: "I'll get there by five o'clock if I break my neck for it." Fast times were popular all round, and were used prominently in promotional material by the competing companies. Rival ships would indeed 'race' to be the first to dock in St Peter Port.

STELLA

Stella sailed at 11.25am, down the Solent and out past the Needles, with the weather fine. From there it was a straight course of 64 miles to the Casquets near Alderney, the only obstacle before entering St Peter Port. It was necessary to set a course which took into account the strength and direction of the tide, allowing safe passage to the west of the Casquets.

Well into the voyage, fog patches became a problem. At the first thick bank of fog, *Stella* slowed to 12 knots. After about 12 minutes it cleared and she resumed full speed. Soon she ran into another bank of fog, and she slowed for 8 minutes. When visibility returned, the captain resumed a speed of 18 knots. When the ship ran into a third fog bank it was thicker and visibility varied by the moment. Stella continued this time at full speed with her fog whistle sounding.

Captain Reeks was familiar with the area, but his confidence about his position was misplaced. At 4pm, without any warning, the bridge, the lookout and many passengers were looking up through gaps in the fog at rocks towering 15-25m above. It must have been terrifying. The captain ordered "full speed astern" and swung the wheel to starboard. *Stella* scraped the first rock mass and ran along another. The fatal injury came next as her 1058 tons drove at 18 knots across the top of a submerged ridge of granite. The violence of the impact shook even the engines from their bed plates, and in less than 10 minutes the vessel sank in deep water.

The boats were put out quickly, and it is reported that passengers were amazingly calm. This calmness may in fact have cost lives as the ship sank very fast and it is estimated that between 86 and 101 people lost their lives. A proper record had not been made of who was on board. Those who managed to get into lifeboats and survive the cold and fearful night drifting up and down the Channel were picked up the next day; a long time to wait for help.

The Guernsey Evening Press of 1 April 1899 said it was extraordinary that news of *Stella* did not reach Guernsey until 8am the day after the wreck (16 hours later). It called for greater safety in future, rather than greater speed. There had been no safety drill or instruction on board, and lifebelts were not always put on correctly.

An enquiry in London concluded on 5 May with three main findings: Reeks did not navigate his ship in a seamanlike manner; disaster was caused by not making the course that was set; and travelling at a high speed in fog when the captain must have known they were somewhere near

the Casquets. No comment was made about 'racing'. The disaster resulted from the captain's over-confidence rather than recklessness.

The captain had calculated a westward drift of 7 miles on the crossing because of the ebbing tide down the Channel, yet *Stella* drifted only 5.5 miles, not enough to miss the Casquets. It is not clear why. She was also 4 miles further forward of where the captain thought she was. This may have been due to not starting the log line correctly - it had become tangled near the Needles.

In 1899 there was no technology available to even consider a dive on such a deep wreck, so it was not until June 1973 that divers Richard Keen and Fred Shaw found Stella sitting upright on the seabed. It had previously been thought that she had sunk at the foot of the rocks, but she was on sand well to the south. It was a dangerous dive to 49m in tidal waters that allowed only 10-15 minutes on the wreck.

FIND OUT MORE

In 1994 a diver from Jersey, John Ovenden, began filming and produced a 50-minute video '*The Wreck of the Stella*'. David Shayer, from Guernsey, teamed up with him in writing and publishing the thoroughly researched book '*The Wreck of the Stella, Titanic of the Channel Islands.*'

IBEX

JANUARY 5, 1900

Struck the Platte Fougere reef just north of Guernsey, and sank near the Roustel Beacon.

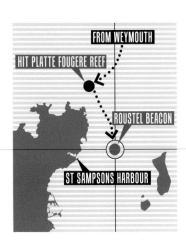

Ibex was built in Birkenhead in 1891, and with twin-screws for speed she once held the channel-crossing record. However, she had the misfortune to be wrecked twice in less than three years.

Her first wrecking was on 16 April 1897 off Jersey. The two steamer companies on the route still engaged in unofficial racing to beat the tides and maintain prestige. This was avoided later by separation on the timetable. On this occasion as *Ibex* left Guernsey she was ten minutes ahead of *Frederica*, but nearing the Corbiere lighthouse in Jersey, with passengers on deck cheering, the two were almost parallel. A risky situation was made worse by the fact that with the tide falling it was only 35 minutes until the harbour would have dried out too far for them to dock. The first ship in would effectively block the other one out. With the rival captains pushing each other to alter course, move over, give way, *Ibex* was forced onto the Noirmontaise rock. No lives were lost. She was towed to the beach at St Aubin's Bay

and was out of service for three months for repairs in England.

Ibex was wrecked again, in 1900, this time off Guernsey on the night crossing from Weymouth with John Baudains as captain. She set out at 2.30am on 5 January with 34 passengers, mail, and 60 tons of cargo. It was a smooth crossing and the ferry passed the Casquets at 5.39am. About half an hour later the leading lights for St Peter Port harbour were spotted. Belvedere, the upper light, was new, and Baudains did not trust it. It was his practice instead to use an unorthodox approach to the harbour which involved a quick turn to port in order to take a bearing on the Casquets 15 miles behind. On this occasion there followed nine minutes of muddled

RACING

SS *Ibex* (Great Western Railway) and
SS *Lydia* (London and South Western Railway)
passing the Casquets in rough weather, 1901.

G.W. Williamson

IBEX

orders and misunderstandings between captain and helmsman which resulted in Ibex striking the south end of the Platte Fougere reef on her starboard side. She had been off course by as much as 40 degrees to the west. Baudains headed for Herm to try to beach the ship there, but the bow went under and she was sinking. He changed his mind and headed for St Sampson's harbour instead, but she sank near the Roustel beacon.

The Star newspaper reported that there had been rumours of a collision and people had seen the vessel's lights from the White Rock, although many passengers on board were unaware of what had happened until called on deck and given lifebelts. Discipline was good, but one passenger and one of the crew drowned. The Harbour Master of St Sampson's went out in a fishing boat to see if the beacon on the Platte was still in place (there was no lighthouse there until 1909). Ibex was in the main channel, a danger to shipping, so red lights were placed on her and shipping

was warned. All possessions and mail bags went down with the ship, as conditions proved very difficult for divers attempting to retrieve things. Spring tides at 6 knots allowed only two hours for diving. It was decided to try to salvage her after the winter when the weather improved.

During much of June and July there were salvage attempts, with delays due to blasting rock to put cables under the hull, broken cables, unhelpful tides and poor weather. On 21 July salvors were successful in raising Ibex and taking her into St Peter Port harbour to be pumped out and repaired. She was a strange sight after six months in the sea, with decks all covered in seaweed. On 26 July the Star said that 'a considerable quantity of jewellery consigned to local dealers has been recovered.'

Ibex continued to serve the islands until 1925, 34 years altogether, and she was held in high regard for her eventful life and loyal service.

Neil Warner, Warner Corporate Photography, Galway

THE STORY OF A RING

Ibex was carrying a gold and diamond engagement ring which the author's grandmother had sent to London for repair. It was being returned, in a lead-lined mail container, when it went to the bottom of the Russel with *Ibex*. Fortunately it was found in one of the recovered mail bags, and delivered to her six months later. In the meantime her husband had given her a replacement ring, not expecting to see the original again. They had the *Ibex* ring engraved on the inside with the words 'Lost Ibex Jan. 5th '00. Found Aug. 16th' plus a three-word inscription in Latin which is now illegible. This ring eventually came to their granddaughter in Galway.

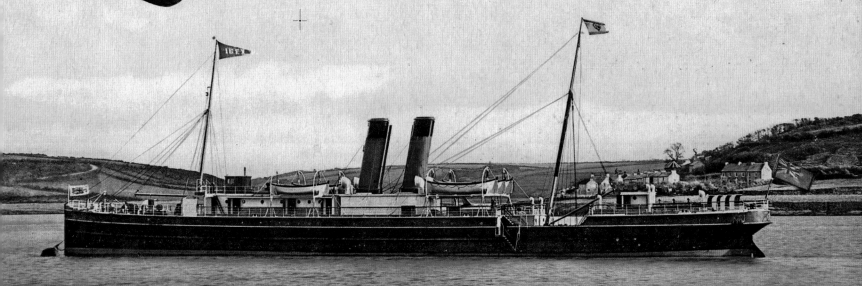

LIVERPOOL

FEBRUARY 25, 1902

Ran on to a rocky ledge at Fort Homeaux Florains on the north east tip of Alderney.

The wreck of *Liverpool* in 1902 saw the largest sailing vessel in the world fighting the fastest tidal stream in Europe. She was built on the Clyde in 1889, made of steel, weighed 3,396 tons, was 101 metres in length, and had a crew of 35. *Liverpool* carried four masts with squared sail yards on all four. Tides around Alderney run counter-clockwise for roughly 9 hours, then clockwise for three hours every 12. The wild Alderney Race can reach 8 knots and there are heavy overfalls, and a sailing ship can be helpless in these conditions.

Liverpool had loaded a mixed cargo of luxury goods in Antwerp on 23 February and was bound for San Francisco. She went through the Straits of Dover and dropped the pilot at 1am on the 24th near the Varne lightship. She passed 19 miles off Beachy Head at 3am. The wind was very light so the English master, Owen Lewis, set full sail to catch every bit of breeze.

The ship took a west-south-west course down the Channel and by 8pm the Barfleur

light near Cherbourg could be seen. The estimated position was 16-18 miles off the point, and the light was still visible at midnight. The wind dropped even more, and *Liverpool* was making only two knots. It was calm and humid, and a light mist was developing into a thick fog.

Estimating the ship's speed was unreliable when making less than four knots. A lookout was posted and soundings were taken regularly from 3.30am on the 25th: no bottom at 60 fathoms, then rocky bottom at 40 fathoms, then 36 fathoms. The captain adjusted course slightly.

LIVERPOOL

The fog was so thick that the crew could not even see the length of the ship. The captain held course, blowing the foghorn. Suddenly the lookout spotted breakers. The captain again ordered a change of course, but the huge vessel could not respond sufficiently at such a slow speed.

At some time after 10am *Liverpool* ran on to a rocky ledge at Fort Homeaux Florains on the north east tip of Alderney, her bow resting on the ledge and her stern dipping. There was no need to abandon ship because she was sitting upright in calm conditions in the fog, all sails eerily set. It was an hour after high spring tide. Ten years later, in 1912, the Quesnard lighthouse was built on this point.

A man who was working at the nearby quarry thought he had seen something strange in the fog. He walked over to investigate and was amazed at what he saw just 100 metres from shore.

He told the crew where they were, and then he and others helped unload some of the cargo as at low tide it was possible to walk to her from the shore. It is said that there was much merriment when cognac was found amongst the cargo.

In spite of looting and drunkenness, much of the cargo not damaged by seawater was salved. Guards were put on the ship to keep a tally of what was landed. The initial optimism about refloating the ship was dashed when it was realised how dangerous the tides and currents were. At high tide four metres of water covered her stern. By the second day her hatches had burst, and the water rushing in flushed out much of the remaining cargo which then floated about.

It was established at the enquiry which was held in Liverpool in May that the ship was probably on a correct course until she entered the influence of the Alderney Race. This very strong current was running at full speed on a spring high tide, and the slow moving *Liverpool* was pulled south into the flow. When she struck the coast of Alderney she was 12 miles south-south-east of her proper course.

The enquiry said of the captain that he had done almost everything correctly (lookout and soundings) but did not accurately know his speed and he had failed to take into account the effect of the dangerous currents in this part of the English Channel. He was allowed to keep his certificate.

The attempt to get *Liverpool* off the rocks failed but most of the cargo was recovered. The ship was sold for £250 to a group from Guernsey who collected up more of the cargo and fittings which made £10,000 at auction in Guernsey. By January 1903 the ship had broken up.

This marble is believed
to be ballast taken from
the *Liverpool* wreck

DUNSINANE

AUGUST 13, 1904

Drifted onto Black Rock, under Vale Castle, after leaving St Sampsons harbour.

BLACK ROCK

ST SAMPSONS HARBOUR

'The finest vessel sailing out of Guernsey' became a spectacular and much-photographed wreck. Built in Dundee in 1874, *Dunsinane* was a 3-masted barquentine, 40m in length, and weighing 253 tons. She regularly carried general cargo to and from Guernsey.

On 13 August 1904 Guernsey was enjoying a fine summer's day, warm with very little wind. *Dunsinane* had been loading 500 tons of good quality granite, and at 7.30pm she eased her way out of the narrows of St Sampson's harbour heading for London.

Captain P Mahy was in command, and the ship belonged to his company P Mahy & Co. He must have expected enough wind to take his ship out into the Russel, but he may not have reckoned on the tide. At this time the tide was very strong, running north.

As soon as *Dunsinane* cleared the breakwater, she was caught in the flow and drifted helplessly onto the Black Rock under Vale Castle. Almost immediately the tide began to ebb so all efforts to free her were futile. All on board, including the captain's wife and child, were landed safely.

The ship was stranded 300m from shore, and was lying across two rocks. At first it was thought the stones could be off-loaded so that the ship would float on the next high tide. This idea had to be abandoned due to the sharp angle of the vessel which had taken on a heavy list to starboard. The Star newspaper suggested that a perpendicular line from her topmast would have hung at least 12m away from the hull. As the tide fell further it was clear how much damage had been caused. One rock had snapped the keel and another had penetrated the bilge.

Although the vessel was insured, the cargo was not. During the next few days the stone was removed by taking

up planking to open the hull. Men were
employed to load carts which went
up and down the beach at low tide to
retrieve the granite. Masts and shrouds
were cut away leaving the hull bare.

Dunsinane was sold for £13 to a
Mr MacPherson of South Shields.
She was then broken up for scrap.

F. W. Guerin

BRISEIS

OCTOBER 1, 1937

Struck Les Grunes reef and sank a mile from Vazon Bay.

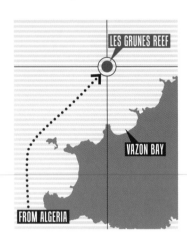

LES GRUNES REEF

VAZON BAY

FROM ALGERIA

C. Toms

The wreck of *Briseis* is one shipwreck story that is remembered with amusement. No lives were lost, and the way islanders raided its cargo of Algerian wine made for a Guernsey version of 'Whisky Galore'.

Briseis was 23 years old at the time of the wreck, having been built in Rostock in 1914 as *Genua*. She was a cargo steam ship of 3000 tons which after the Great War was acquired by the Companie Auxiliare de Navigation, a French trading company. Captain Le Hellidu knew her well, as he had been her master for many years. The passage was from Oran in Algeria to Rouen, the historic capital of Normandy on the Seine. The cargo was phosphates and 7000 casks of wine.

The first of October 1937 was a quiet calm day in Guernsey, with a slight haze as *Briseis* passed the Hanois and hugged the west coast far too tightly. People watching at Richmond, Vazon and Cobo were amazed at her course, dangerously inshore for such a

ship. They saw her bow rise up as she struck Les Grunes reef. There was an attempt to turn the ship to starboard and dash for Vazon to beach her, but halfway there the ship's siren was heard and the bow slipped under the water - when she was still a mile from shore.

The Guernsey Weekly Press said it was 'tragic and fascinating, a steamer going down in a mighty cascade of steam, smoke and water'. All 27 crewmen took to the boats, and other boats put out from Vazon. The lifeboat was called and in 15 minutes she was leaving the harbour.

C. Toms

BRISEIS

C. Toms

CURIOUS PARALLEL

In a curious parallel to the story of *Briseis*, Compton McKenzie wrote 'Whisky Galore' in 1947 inspired by *SS Politician* wrecked on the Scottish island of Eriskay in 1941 with a cargo of whisky. It was made into a film in 1949.

Very soon there were about 300 barrels of Algerian wine floating around in the bay, and islanders were quick to respond to the rumour. For many people the gift of wine was just too tempting. It is said that there were scenes of lusty drunkenness on the beach as casks were broken open and the juice was sucked or poured into thirsty throats. A few people even managed to bring wine glasses.

Looting went on all day, and that night a mystery boat apparently stood by *Briseis* prompting the police to call on boatmen to give chase to the looters. An official warning was issued saying that all goods salved must be declared immediately. Later, 50 barrels were handed in from as far away as St Martin's point and even some floating off towards Sark.

The wreck of *Briseis* lies in shallow water at a depth of 15m–23m depending on the tide. She is on her port side, intact but flattened. The large boilers and engine block are still there, and it is considered to be a good dive site with lots of marine life.

C. Toms

HMS CHARYBDIS & HMS LIMBOURNE

OCTOBER 23, 1943

Struck by torpedoes and sunk south of Guernsey.

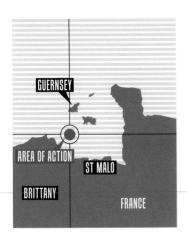

GUERNSEY

AREA OF ACTION

ST MALO

BRITTANY

FRANCE

Men lost from these two Royal Navy ships during 1943 are buried in Guernsey, although the ships were attacked and sunk some distance south of its coasts. The Channel Islands were occupied by the Germans, and the incident deeply affected islanders during that dark time. It was one of the worst disasters in the Channel during the Second World War, with over 500 men lost from the two ships.

Charybdis was a cruiser and *Limbourne* a destroyer. A small British task force would regularly sweep the coast of Brittany for German convoys trying to slip at night along the French coast from Brest to Cherbourg via St Malo. Although *Charybdis* had only just completed a successful campaign in the Mediterranean, she was brought in on this occasion to add punch to a special operation. The large German merchant ship *Munsterland* was in Brest ready to run vital supplies, and a RAF bombing raid had failed to sink her in the harbour. On the night of 22-23 October 1943 *Charybdis* joined two Fleet destroyers and four Hunt class destroyers

Bell from the sixth ship named *HMS Charybdis* commissioned in 1969. The bell rope was made by a survivor of the 1943 attack.

including *Limbourne* to try to intercept the German ship. The flotilla left Plymouth blacked out and in radio silence, sailing in single line-ahead formation.

Cloudy and misty weather, with fine rain, made for poor visibility. From just north of Sept Iles at 0030 hours they began to sweep to the west at 13 knots. The British

HMS Charybdis

were unaware that *Munsterland* and 11 escorts were close, or that German coastal radar had already detected them. *Charybdis* began picking up German radio signals, but there was considerable confusion and no precise location. She ordered the British group to turn slightly to starboard and to increase speed to 18 knots. Because of radio problems only one ship received this message.

By 0142 hours, as *Charybdis* became isolated ahead of her group, German torpedo boats came within visual range, closing in at 27 knots. Six torpedoes were fired at *Charybdis* in a fan formation, white tracks were seen approaching, and there was a massive explosion. Some crew were thrown overboard, some killed immediately, and the ship began listing. At 0155 hours, less than 20

minutes since first radar contact, *Charybdis* was lost. The order was given to "abandon ship" but there was no power for the cranes to launch the lifeboats. As the listing increased quickly from 10 degrees to 45 degrees she disappeared in a sea of bodies and burning oil.

Within minutes, another tragedy struck. *Limbourne* was hit by a

HMS CHARYBDIS & HMS LIMBOURNE

David Le Cheminant
2012

torpedo at 0157 hours which blew up her forward magazine and removed her bow. As she was drifting towards the French coast she was taken in tow, but could be moved only in circles. At 0640 she was sunk to keep her out of enemy hands.

In retrospect it became clear that this operation was deeply flawed. The task force had no collective training, and they used the wrong formation for these circumstances. It sailed with whatever ships happened to be available, with *Charybdis* too large for an operation more suited to destroyers.

On 15 November, three weeks later, the Guernsey Evening Press reported that bodies were being washed ashore. In total 21 were recovered for burial in Guernsey and the verdicts were 'found

drowned'. More bodies washed up on the other islands and in France.

The occupying authorities in Guernsey allowed a burial service with full naval honours to be open to the public. On 17 November some 5,000 islanders, a quarter of the remaining population, joined the service at the Foulon Cemetery. The Press said 'mourning became international' and over 900 wreaths and sprays were placed beside the graves, 'the greatest array of wreaths ever seen in the island'. The Germans realised that 'the heart knows no frontiers' but they were not expecting this powerful silent symbol of island feeling. It came to represent a quiet statement of loyalty to Britain and its forces in the face of Nazi oppression. Such a ceremony was not permitted in Jersey. An annual '*Charybdis* Day' memorial service is still held each autumn, and Royal Naval personnel are traditionally in attendance.

Diving on these wrecks is quite deep and dangerous, but in 1993 *Charybdis* was found at 82m, and in 2002 *Limbourne* was found at 80m. Both were surprisingly clear of corrosion and marine growth.

ernsey Press

ernsey Press

FIND OUT MORE

The graves of sailors from
Charybdis and *Limbourne*
lie in the Foulon cemetery
on the western outskirts
of St Peter Port. The
headstones reveal the
hard truth that some of
the dead were still in
their teens.

FERMAIN

DECEMBER 29, 1952

Blown on to Black Rock, under Vale Castle, after leaving St Sampsons harbour.

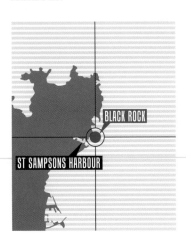

Like *Dunsinane* in 1904, *Fermain* was caught out in 1952 by the tricky entrance to St Sampson's harbour: narrow, rocks nearby, and with strong cross-wind and tide. *Fermain*, 1,086 tons, was owned by O. Dorey & Sons, and she had sailed from Swansea carrying 1,300 tons of Welsh anthracite, the all-important fuel at that time for heating the Guernsey tomato greenhouses.

A flood tide and gale-force winds on 29 December meant that *Fermain* delayed going in to the harbour, and for most of the day she had been at anchor in the roads between Jethou and Guernsey. The captain was on leave, so a stand-in was on duty. A local pilot went on board, and soon after 5pm the collier tried to enter the harbour to unload. Moving carefully under reduced power, she was carried by the force of the wind and tide pushing against her port side onto the infamous Black Rock. This dangerous rock is on the short stretch

of coast between Fort Doyle and Mont Crevelt which has claimed at least 12 ships.

The St Sampson's pilot boat, *Dolphin*, made three trips to take off some crew and belongings, and at 5.20pm the St Peter Port lifeboat was launched. The crew were landed and accommodated at Moore's Hotel in town.

As if to emphasise the importance of fuel to the local tomato industry, the wreck was sold before 8 January 1953 to a firm whose aim was to salvage the coal and then break up the hull for scrap. It was necessary to do this quickly before the sea broke up the ship. A temporary causeway was constructed from the coast road to the ship, and a large hole was cut in her side, so that lorries could drive at low tide right up to and into the hull to bring the coal ashore.

This all took some days and there was a nervousness about getting the job done

in time. By 16 January the 230-metre causeway was complete, and the race against time and tide continued. Men worked with lights at night from 2-6am, and the coal was dumped in a yard on the south side of Vale Castle. The Guernsey Evening Press reported that 600 tons had been saved by 2 February. Meanwhile, local people carried on hunting for ormers in rock-pools nearby.

RAF SUNDERLAND

SEPTEMBER 15, 1954

Hit submerged rock outside St Peter Port Harbour and then towed to safety.

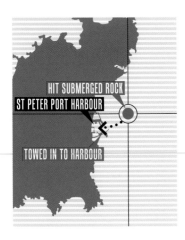

HIT SUBMERGED ROCK
ST PETER PORT HARBOUR

TOWED IN TO HARBOUR

In addition to shipwrecks, the waters around Guernsey are the last resting place of dozens of aircraft shot down during the Second World War. The most famous aircraft wreck however happened in peacetime.

On 14 September 1954 a special lunch party was held at the Old Government House Hotel in St Peter Port to mark the arrival in the island of two Sunderland flying boats which were attached to No. 201 Squadron RAF. The Squadron had been associated with the island since 1939 and was known as 'Guernsey's Own'. RAF personnel on board included men intending to play a football match in the island. In his welcome speech, the Bailiff said he thought it would be a good idea if the Squadron visited the island on Liberation Day on 9 May. The Guernsey Evening Press reported that it was an excellent lunch with fine speeches and loyal toasts.

Next day, 15 September, there was a dramatic accident when one of the flying boats hit a submerged rock when landing outside the harbour mouth at St Peter Port.

Amazingly, twenty-three personnel escaped. There were no lives lost, and no injuries reported.

Many small boats rushed to the scene and towed the £250,000 flying boat into the inner harbour. RAF personnel worked through the night with the help of powerful floodlights. A full inspection revealed a slit along the bottom of the fuselage. It seemed to be repairable, and specialist engineers arrived from England to examine her further.

A surprising aspect of this incident was that a Guernsey girl was on board. At 19 years of age, and in the Women's Royal Air Force, she was a leading aircraft woman based in Plymouth. She had permission from her commanding officer to travel home to Guernsey on the Sunderland for this occasion.

The flying boat was moved further up to the Careening Hard, and it was decided that special cement was needed for the hull, and the engines would have to be replaced.

el Toms

On 17 September the Press reported that after 'splendid salvage work' she was now seaworthy. 2.5 tons of cement and sand were used on the hull to cover the 8m-9m slit. As she floated on the tide, she was pulled further up the Hard. The floats were pumped out, and the fuel tanks were emptied and washed out of seawater. The engines were taken out and four new ones brought in. The plane was then able to fly back to England.

FIND OUT MORE

The 201 Squadron (RAF) Museum is located at Castle Cornet and includes memorabilia, models and photographs telling the history of the squadron from 1914 until its disbandment in 2012.

LA SALLE

MAY 28, 1965

Struck the Grunes reef off Vazon and sank after coming to rest on rocks.

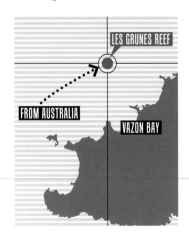

The weather was fair on 28 May 1965 with a light to moderate south-westerly. Weather was not a factor when *La Salle* started flashing urgent morse code messages at 4.45am. She had hit the Soufleurese and Le Boin rocks in the Grunes reef off Vazon before coming to rest with a hole in the engine-room.

La Salle was a Liberian-registered cargo vessel weighing 4560 tons. Her crew of 40 included 30 Chinese and the rest were mainly Dutch. She was carrying timber and oats from South Australia to Cape Town and on to Hamburg.

The lifeboat was soon on her way to the west coast where *La Salle* was visible to people who were already gathering in the mist along the Perelle road. Early morning radio bulletins were telling the island what was happening. She was sitting on the reef, stern raised, bow under water, and her back was broken.

Richard Colin Le Marquand

Although there was a bit of swell, the crew simply climbed over the side of the wreck into the lifeboat and all 40 were saved. The Panamanian tug *Cintra* arrived to see if *La Salle* could be pulled off the reef, but there was no hope of saving the vessel with three breaks in her back.

The Star newspaper reported on 29 May that "looters" had been on board. The Dutch second mate had returned to the ship to fetch papers, and he saw that someone had tried to open the food, wine and tobacco stores with tyre levers.

Oil was escaping from the wreck on 30 May, so 200 gallons of a special oil-dispersal detergent was rushed to the island and sprayed on the sea around *La Salle*.

By the 8 June *La Salle* sunk further and was breaking up. Quantities of timber were floating about posing a threat especially to fast boats, so a warning was issued to the ferry *Condor I* and speed boats about this danger. There were reports of timber being carried away in vans and hand-carts.

Brehaut

PRESIDENT GARCIA

JULY 13, 1967

Steamed in to Saints Bay at 12 knots and collided with rocks at the base of the cliffs.

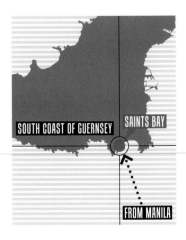

It was a very warm pleasant day on 13 July 1967 with only light winds, but in the evening it became misty. Shortly before midnight, a courting couple on the south coast at the fishermen's harbour in Saints Bay were surprised to see what appeared to be a large trawler heading for the Peastacks. She then turned in towards Moulin Huet Bay without slowing down at all. *President Garcia* came on to Saints Bay and loomed out of the mist towards the slipway at 12 knots, and its 7,687 tons crashed into the 100m rocky cliff beside them. The girl put her fingers in her ears but still heard the crunch which "shook the cliff".

President Garcia had miraculously missed hitting most of the small boats moored in the bay. A couple sleeping in a visiting yacht were lucky to be alive as the ship missed them by just two metres.

The courting couple joined two telephone engineers working nearby and hurried up the little valley to raise the alarm.

In the nearest pub nobody could believe their story and thought they were practical jokers. Finally they were taken seriously, and after a phone call the lifeboat was on its way.

Built in 1942 in Seattle, *President Garcia* had begun life as a cargo ship, then been converted to an escort aircraft carrier with 24 aircraft for convoy escort duties with the Royal Navy. She was back in the US in 1946, in Argentina in 1948, and finally in the Philippines in 1965 where she was owned by Philippine President Lines.

Richard Colin Le Marquand

PRESIDENT GARCIA

Priaulx Library

President Garcia had left Manila 42 days earlier with a cargo of copra (dried coconut valued for its oil) bound for Rotterdam. Her crew evidently mistook St Martin's Point for the Hanois, and thinking she had cleared the south-west of the island, headed north and straight into the bay. The bow was stuck fast from the impact, with the stern lying on the sandy bottom. As it was high tide, there was no further lift coming, and she would not budge.

A Dutch tug, the lifeboat, and a couple of trawlers stood by in case help was needed. The public had to be kept away from the fishermen's harbour, but crowds gathered on the cliff tops on either side of the bay. There was silence, no panic, and the crew stood on deck looking up at the cliffs. The captain maintained a strict silence with the public, but crew members spoke of the radar being out of order.

The 53 crew initially remained on board while attempts were made to move her. The Dutch tug was unable to move the ship even with the help of the ship's propellers, so divers investigated where she was being held. If a southerly wind arose, it would break her up. Two days after the grounding, some of the copra was removed to lighten the vessel and give her the necessary buoyancy. The crew were allowed ashore but every one of them had to agree to leave Guernsey with the ship.

Copra beetles escaped from the cargo and flew ashore. This is a significant pest which is 4-6 millimetres long, and bluish-green in colour. They were seen at Petit Bot and in gardens along the Jerbourg road, but did not survive for long.

After a week in Saints Bay the wrecked ship slid off the rocks and was towed to anchor off St Peter Port harbour. Oil leaks were repaired and more copra was unloaded. She was towed to Rotterdam in three days, surveyed in dry dock, but was declared a constructive total loss.

ELWOOD MEAD

DECEMBER 25, 1973

Struck the Grunes reef off Vazon and became stuck on the rocks.

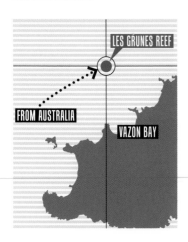

LES GRUNES REEF

FROM AUSTRALIA

VAZON BAY

Rio Tinto owns one of the biggest mining operations in the world, in the Pilbara region of Western Australia, where very long trains haul iron ore to the coast at Dampier. In some years they mine over 200 million tonnes, about 13% of world production.

From Dampier a fleet of large bulk carriers transport the ore across the globe. In 1973 the very biggest of these, *Elwood Mead*, which had been built in Hiroshima, was loading up for her maiden voyage to Rotterdam. She was registered in Monrovia, the capital of Liberia, and was 260m long, 40m wide, with a draught of 16m, and weighed 59,192 tons. Her ten self-contained holds carried 122,954 tons of iron ore (enough to make 30,000 cars), and she and her cargo were worth over £10 million.

After 33 days at sea she entered the Channel intending to pick up a pilot at Cherbourg for the tricky final part of the voyage. The sea was rough, although

nothing too much for a ship of her size to handle, but errors in navigation coupled with the weather resulted in *Elwood Mead* coming too far south and striking Les Grunes at 4am on Christmas Day 1973. The super-freighter spent 61 days on rocks off the west coast of Guernsey.

Two ocean-going tugs were soon on the scene. Some 12 of the 34 crew were put ashore and taken to Moore's Hotel in St Peter Port. She was carrying 750 tons of heavy oil and 150 tons of light oil for the engines, so there was a risk of pollution. The Dutch experts Wijsmuller were given the salvage contract on a 'no cure, no pay' basis.

During the last days of December the salvors worked as quickly as possible because of fears of oil spillage in the face of an approaching westerly Force 8. Decks were sprayed with detergent, and a 12-man team arrived from Amsterdam with 6 tons of salvage equipment. There were high winds and a heavy swell, and no imminent spring tides which would help lift the ship. Seven days after the accident the salvors were hoping to try a lift, but if that did not work they would have to wait for bigger tides. Compressed air was pumped into some tanks for extra lift, and unloading some cargo was considered.

B. W. Currell

ELWOOD MEAD

Guernsey Press

The Guernsey Evening Press noted that this was the most expensive maiden voyage since *Titanic*. Underwater photographs showed the damaged plates of the outer skin and the fractured oil tanks, but the inner hull plates were sound. More equipment, valued at £27,000, was brought in, and there was quiet confidence about a refloating attempt on 2 January 1974. A survey had found a safe passage avoiding rocks for the giant vessel to take once she was afloat and had been turned to face deep water. All was ready.

This first attempt failed. Pinnacles of rock were embedded in the hull, and although lift was achieved it was not enough. The bow was moved around by 7 degrees, but 5,000 tons of water flooded the 4-storey engine room. Experts from America were called in to prevent rusting of the engines. The wind strength increased to Force 9.

By 6 January only the master and his first officer were still on board. It was freezing cold as the main heating system had been turned off. The ship had been forced back onto the seabed in order to sit out the storm which was now Force 10.

On 9 January it was decided to remove some of the ore as there was a 7m swell running the full length of the hull. A Wessex helicopter was called in to lift heavy equipment onto the deck. Cracks of 2cm-22cm were appearing between hatches numbers 2 and 7.

STILL ON THE SEABED

Abandoned somewhere on the seabed at the Grunes are 15 tons of tackle at a depth of 20m, over 300m of cable, and an anchor weighing 12 tons.

Iron ore was pumped out into the sea to lighten the ship and on 20 January the Polish captain, Robert Nowryta, left the ship for the first time. He returned on board four days later for the duration of the salvage. The target for the next big lift was 9 February, so preparations continued. Weather was causing difficulties and there was some further damage to the ship. 15,000 tons of ore had been pumped overboard, but water had got into holds 2 and 8. The second attempt to lift her off was prevented by the weather.

A race against time began to get ready for the next opportunity on 23-25 February. Holds 6 and 7 were too damaged to repair on the spot. Ballast water was reduced from 80,000 to 40,000 tons: any less might have made the ship too lively. A lift of 4.5m was needed to clear the rock pinnacles which were holding her. With four ocean-going tugs, and ground tackle to hold her firm, a third attempt failed at 7am on 22 February. A fourth in the evening also failed. Oil escaped onto the beach at Vazon and Portelet.

Finally, at 8.45am on 24 February 1974, *Elwood Mead* was successfully refloated. The four big tugs were still in place, as well as two onboard winches pulling at massive anchors laid on the seabed by the salvage ship *Krab*. The salvage company was responsible for the safety of the ship until she was in dry dock in Rotterdam. In all, 25,000 tons of her cargo was dumped. The plan was that she would be moored for two days in a calm location for a complete survey of the hull, but the weather prevented this, so she was towed directly away to Rotterdam. While the huge ship made her way up the Channel, two ships came perilously close to her in the night, and lights were flashed at them. Off the Hook of Holland more ore was off-loaded into barges. Divers found one hole measuring 20m x 5m. Eventually she was re-fitted and re-named *Good Leader*.

A formal enquiry in London was set up to look at marine traffic in the shipping lanes west of Guernsey. It included representatives from Guernsey, Trinity House, and the Department of Trade and Industry.

PROSPERITY

JANUARY 16, 1974

Struck the Conchee reef off Perelle after breaking down 20 miles west of the Hanois.

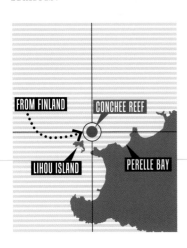

The wreck of *Prosperity* is Guernsey's deadliest maritime tragedy of recent times, with 18 lives lost on the night of 16-17 January 1974. *Prosperity* was an ageing Cypriot ship, built in 1943, taking a cargo of timber planks from Finland to Pireaus in Greece. The crew was multinational, including men from India, Africa, Pakistan, Turkey and Greece, aged from 45 to 16. One woman was also on board: assistant steward Gloria Pangratis, wife of the second engineer.

Weather was a key factor in this wreck, with severe gale/storm force winds in one of the worst storms ever recorded by the Met Office. *Prosperity* broke down in mid-Channel during the afternoon. She was about 20 miles west of the Hanois when the Greek master, Kastellorizias, sent out a distress call that said "the engine had failed and the vessel was going round and round without power". With mountainous seas all around, it was too dangerous to abandon ship.

Richard Keen

The lifeboat *Sir William Arnold* put to sea in horrendous conditions, and there was almost zero visibility along the south coast with spray from the 8-metre waves. She was limited to less than half her top speed. *Prosperity* had radioed for a tug and a lifeboat, but at 6.20pm the master radioed again to say his crew were preparing to abandon ship.

At 9.15pm the lifeboat was 8 miles south west of the Hanois, but nothing could be seen, and at that point the coxswain and the harbour master agreed to abandon the rescue mission. They believed there was no reasonable chance of finding anyone on board *Prosperity*, and nothing had been heard from the ship for nearly three hours.

W. Currell

PROSPERITY

During the night *Prosperity* crashed into the Conchee reef off Perelle, probably without any crew on board by this time. She broke into two pieces, and the timber was washed out of the ship and floated off. All this time the *Elwood Mead* was herself still wedged on rocks further north.

The wreck was first found by police officers who were patrolling by car early in the morning on 17 January. The 2100-ton vessel was visible in the headlights. The lifeboat was launched again at 6.30am, and at 8.15am she was on site. A French Lockheed patrol aircraft also assisted in the search. The Guernsey Press said that with the Force 11 winds a plane flying at 120 metres over the scene had sea-spray on the windscreen. Tragically, there were no survivors at all. Later that day 16 bodies, all wearing lifejackets, were recovered from the sea near the Hanois lighthouse. Two men, including the captain, were never found. It remains a mystery whether the crew had jumped into the sea or had taken to a lifeboat that was then lost.

The inquest recorded a verdict of misadventure. The local community was touched by the enormity of this accident, and two funds were set up. One was to help the families, and the other to build a lasting memorial. This is now by the car park on Lihou headland, widely known as the 'Prosperity Car Park'.

As for the 2,250 tons of top-quality timber planks, most was washed up on west coast beaches. When islanders turned up in large numbers to rescue it, the Receiver of Wreck issued a warning

in the Press that it was not legal to keep it and all timber should be brought to the States Works yard at La Charroterie. Norman Piette Ltd put in a successful bid for that timber, however much of the cargo simply disappeared around the island.

Prosperity slipped off the reef and settled on the seabed. She is now all but destroyed, but parts of her boiler can still be seen at very low tide.

Margaret Broad

BIG APPLE

JUNE 14, 1977

Struck a rock and grounded near the Beaucette marina entrance.

The most successful designer of ocean-racing yachts in the 1970s was a New Zealander called Ron Holland. He began to make a name for himself in Auckland, and then moved to Ireland and settled in Kinsale where a number of high profile yachtsmen asked him to design fantastic racing boats. One of these was *Big Apple*, the 'most out-and-out of racing machines'.

This luxury racing sloop was a 44-footer and cost £85,000, a massive sum for that time. She was the Irish contender for the prestigious Admiral's Cup, the international race based at Cowes. Brand new that season, the 'last word in ocean-racing yachts', she was on a cruise of the Solent and the Channel Islands to test and trial her. She usually carried a crew of eleven, and was unbeaten in all races so far.

On 14 June 1977 the skipper took *Big Apple* out of St Peter Port harbour in order to motor the two miles or so

to Beaucette marina. The sea was calm and there was a light northerly breeze. The skipper tried to enter Beaucette an hour before low water having received instructions from the Signal Station about negotiating the narrow entrance to the marina. He was also consulting a navigation manual, and it was reported that there was some confusion between the two sources about the position of a buoy.

Big Apple hit a rock and grounded near the marina entrance. The crew managed to rescue some of the yacht's expensive gear including radio and navigation equipment, but she could not be towed into deeper water, and was soon abandoned. At high tide next morning she was moved out, but the rising tide had battered her on the port side.

Flotation bags were fitted around the hull, and the yacht was towed back to St Peter Port harbour. She was craned out at the container berth with a heavy-duty crane. The damage was now more visible, with holes and dents in the aluminium hull, and damage to the timber frame. With reference to the hull, some joker painted the word 'crumble' below the boat's name.

Repairs had to be done in England. *Big Apple* left St Peter Port as deck cargo for Portsmouth on 22 June, and then on to Southampton to be repaired. She had been the main hope for July's Admiral Cup Race, but although she was finished for that year she later returned to racing.

Buz White

OIL RIG ORION

FEBRUARY 1, 1978

Broke free from its tow and went aground at Grandes Rocques on the west coast of Guernsey.

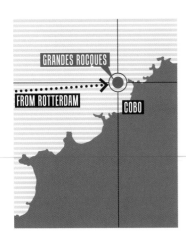

Richard Keen

The wreck of *Orion* must rate as the most spectacular and unusual of all Guernsey wrecks. She was a huge oil rig of 19,000 tons, 76 metres high and worth £10 million, being delivered from Rotterdam to Recife in Brazil. To make the journey she was welded to a specially-prepared barge, *Federal 400-2*, which also carried the rig's equipment valued at £1 million.

On 1 February 1978 the German deep-sea tug *Seefalke* was towing *Orion* into one of the worst winter gales with a west-north-west wind at Force 9. When the heavy tow-line snapped it was not possible to re-attach it, and so *Orion* drifted towards the rocky west coast of Guernsey at six knots. During the evening the 'all ships' Mayday alert was picked up at the St Peter Port signal station. The radio operator immediately contacted the harbour master and the lifeboat, and a full emergency was put in place involving police, fire brigade, ambulance, and hospitals. *Orion* was 21 miles from Guernsey.

The first task was to rescue the 33 men on board before she grounded, and the lifeboat reached *Orion* at 10.50pm. The lifeboatmen had never witnessed anything like the scene of *Orion* with all her lights on 'like a giant Christmas tree'. Two men were taken off by the lifeboat and then Sea King helicopters arrived from Cornwall and rescued another 25, winching them one by one from the rig in winds which were now gusting to Force 12. Conditions were very difficult for the pilots because of the bright lights, the spray and the hurricane winds.

Charles Jaques

73

OIL RIG ORION

Richard Keen

A French helicopter came in to get the final six men, but conditions had deteriorated and the six remained on board overnight. The rig's helipad could not be used as water was breaking over it. *Orion* went aground at 10pm at Grandes Rocques. At 2.15am it was deemed too risky to continue the rescue operation, and at 4.15am the lifeboat returned to the harbour.

At dawn, a St John Ambulance team used breeches-buoy equipment to get two more men off, but helicopters were needed again to complete the job. All the crew were saved in appalling conditions, and the helicopter pilots earned great praise for their skill and bravery. At times rotor blades were within two metres of the rig's giant legs. It was a superb rescue operation according to the chairman of the RNLI, everyone was in the right place at the right time, and much had been learned from the recent emergencies with *Elwood Mead* and *Prosperity*.

The Dutch salvage firm Wijsmuller was given the contract to deal with the valuable oil rig on a 'no cure, no pay' basis. With weather still atrocious there was great urgency because of the risk of the barge crumbling under the weight of the massive rig. By 6 February the wind had eased to Force 5, and a KLM Sikorski helicopter made 11 trips to the rig with 15 tons of salvage equipment, refuelling at the airport. Wijsmuller called in the powerful tug *Typhoon*. The initial plan was to lift the barge with compressed air, but its hull was badly ripped and all tanks were flooded. On 8 February things were not yet ready for the attempt so the very high tide that day was missed. This caused a setback of two weeks. On 9 February it was snowing and the rig was floating above the barge in Force 6-7 winds.

A new plan was devised: to jack up the rig on its four legs, cut the barge into two sections, and use explosives on some of the rock pinnacles which were holding the hull. All preparations were in place on 24 February, but the swell and bad weather were causing delays.

After 25 days, at 8.40am on 27 February, *Orion* was off. The rig was towed away for repairs in Cherbourg which would take a month. The barge was freed on 12 March and was declared a total loss as it would have cost £1.5 million to repair. Another barge was ordered for the crossing to Brazil.

L. G. Timewell

GALLANTRY AWARD

It had been a dramatic rescue operation, and the lifeboat coxswain John Petit received the Silver Medal for gallantry from the RNLI, as well as the RNLI's Maud Smith Award for the bravest act of lifesaving in 1978.

BONITA

DECEMBER 13, 1981

Capsized and sunk
five miles north of the
Channel Lightship in the
English Channel.

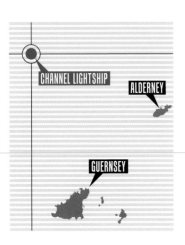

Bonita was a 10,000 ton freighter built in
1970 and registered in Guayaquil, Ecuador.
On 13 December 1981 she was sailing down
the Channel into an intense depression
with hurricane force winds. Her cargo was
fertiliser en route from Hamburg to Panama.
In Guernsey the storm was so severe it broke
windows along Les Banques in St Peter Port.

Bonita was in the busy westward shipping
lane when two massive rogue waves struck
her and she capsized. Listing heavily and
in danger of sinking, she radioed for help
about five miles north of the Channel
Lightship. The wing of her bridge was
dipping into the sea.

The St Peter Port lifeboat *Sir William
Arnold* was quickly on the scene, as the
lifeboatmen were already at the harbour to
move her because of the storm. The lifeboat
was named after a Guernsey Bailiff who
died in office in 1973. The young coxswain,
Mike Scales, was on his first major rescue
mission which was to prove both dangerous
and dramatic.

When the lifeboat reached *Bonita*, the
sea was too rough to go alongside. Ropes
were thrown to the crew, who tied the
rope around their bodies and jumped into
the huge sea. They were hauled through
15m waves to the lifeboat. The terrified
crew did not speak much English, but
nevertheless had to be persuaded to
move from the wheelhouse to the stern
for this operation to work. In all, the
lifeboat made 50 runs to the stern of
the sinking ship. Two men who tried
jumping straight onto the lifeboat were
injured.

Two vessels were standing by in case
they could help. One was a German
freighter called *Charlottenburg* and the

H. Beavis, on loan from RNLI

other was *Olna*, a Royal Fleet Auxiliary tanker. Helicopters were also made available from Royal Navy stations at Culdrose, Portland, and Lee-on-Solent.

The rescue took three hours, and everyone was off *Bonita* before she sank in the wild sea, although one man later died. The lifeboat rescued 28 people, helicopters winched five more crew to safety, and a French tug took off a man with a broken leg. Cold and wet, the crew were taken to Brixham and transferred to Torbay Hospital in Torquay.

Sir William Arnold suffered some superficial damage during the rescue. Large crowds greeted the return of the lifeboat, and the lifeboat crew received a very warm welcome home from the Governor, Peter Le Cheminant.

COGEME - ITECO - 69

Tony Rive

SEPTEMBER 3, 1993

Hit rocks in Belle Greve bay just outside St Peter Port harbour and became grounded.

BELLE GREVE BAY

ST PETER PORT HARBOUR

During the 1980s and early 1990s, Guernsey International Powerboat Week was a high-profile event in the sporting calendar. In 1988 Guernsey issued a set of four stamps to commemorate The World Offshore Powerboat Championships. The powerboats were expensive, colourful and extremely fast. Races were filmed from helicopters, and could be exciting to the point of hair-raising. One particular powerboat experienced two accidents in two days.

Cogeme-Iteco-69 was a 14-metre Class I offshore powerboat with two hulls. Her engines alone cost £60,000 each. This boat was sponsored by two large Italian companies that specialised in electronics and steel. Its drivers were Francesco Pansini and Floriano Omoboni.

On 3 September 1993 the powerboat was being tested in advance of the British Grand Prix when she hit rocks in Belle Greve bay just outside St Peter Port harbour. Not much damage was done,

but there was a falling tide at that time, and soon she was sitting high and dry with the high-tech hull balanced on a rock between the hulls. Memorable photographs showed her nose and engines completely unsupported.

Cogeme was quickly salvaged and made ready for racing on 5 September, when she was eleventh in the running order. In good conditions she was capable of speeds of over 130mph, but off the south of Herm she suffered a serious crash. Reports said she 'entered a spin, and as Pansini attempted to right the boat he hit a wave, sending the boat spiralling forward, entering a barrel-roll before submerging.'

Pansini suffered internal injuries, and Omoboni the co-driver was shocked but otherwise not seriously hurt. The drivers were temporarily trapped as their lifejackets had inflated, and the St John Ambulance divers had difficulty getting them out of the cockpits. Pansini had blood-stained foam at the mouth and was unconscious. Both were rushed to the Princess Elizabeth Hospital on the marine ambulance *Flying Christine*.

The powerboat sank and came to rest upside down at the foot of a reef 200m north-north-west of the Lower Heads buoy at a depth of 36m. An immediate salvage attempt was led by Richard Keen, and his team spent 8 hours searching for the boat and filming in preparation for the lift. She was winched from the seas in 'atrocious weather conditions' which delayed the operation by over two hours. Damage was slight, but the rudder was twisted and there

were some dents on the bodywork. The engines had to be flushed clean of seawater.

On 8 September, *Cogeme's* engines were fired up and working, but she would not race again in that Championship. She was lifted onto the Italian team trailer ready to return home. Pansini was declared 'satisfactory' and was transferred from intensive care to a general ward before also going home.

TRIDENT VI

JUNE 14, 1994

Sank after impact while moored alongside the New Jetty in St Peter Port harbour.

NEW JETTY

ST PETER PORT HARBOUR

Not all accidents happen on the open sea. Just after 6am on 14 June 1994, a large freight carrier entered St Peter Port harbour but did not slow down enough and smashed right into the Sark ferry which was moored against the New Jetty.

Trident VI had been chartered for the summer season by the Sark Shipping Company as the Sark ferry. She was a 250-seater, valued at about £750,000. Nobody was on board, as she was not due to make the first crossing until 8am. *Trident VI* was almost sliced in two, and she sank immediately in the shallow harbour water.

The freight carrier *Norman Commodore* had experienced a fire on board the previous December, and had been in England for refurbishment. This was her first time back in St Peter Port after six months.

Chris George, the Guernsey Evening Press photographer, was on assignment

Guernsey Press

at the harbour to record *Norman Commodore's* return to the island. He was standing on the corner of the New Jetty as the ship came straight towards him. He later said that there was silence, no bow thrusters in use, no panic, then came the sound of timber cracking.

Brian Hayball, master of *Norman Commodore*, said that his ship failed to respond to the controls and there must have been some kind of mechanical fault. He was heading for No.1 ramp but never made it. Although the ship suffered minor damage to the bow,

Tony Rive

nobody was hurt. *Norman Commodore* was inspected, and work was carried out on her port engine and the bow thrusters. The damage to the New Jetty was only superficial and cost about £5,000 to repair.

The hull of *Trident VI* was moved to St Sampson's harbour. The insurers agreed to pay in full, and her damaged sides were re-plated. She was bought back by the previous owners, Travel Trident.

The inquiry found that mechanical failure was the cause of the accident, and that a spring tide and swell in the harbour were also contributory factors.

Guernsey Press

VERMONTBORG

JANUARY 3, 2003

Drifted onto the Capelle reef near Lihou off the west coast of Guernsey.

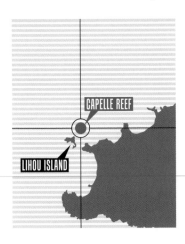

This massive unfitted hull, 120m long, was built in Mangalia in Romania and was being towed via the Black Sea and the Mediterranean to Delfzijl in the north of the Netherlands. She was empty, with no engines and no crew, but carried 200 tonnes of water in ballast. This hull was worth between £1.6 and £2 million.

In January 2003, *Vermontborg* was being towed up the Channel by the tug *Suzanne-H*. The tug was struggling in heavy seas with the huge weight on her tow rope. With hindsight it would have been better not to have crossed Biscay and entered the Channel in such weather. When the rope snapped in the night, *Vermontborg* was set adrift 40-50 miles west of Guernsey. The towing company radioed for helicopters to re-establish the tow, but this was refused by the English and French authorities due to the conditions at sea and because there was no risk to life.

With a strong west-north-west wind pushing her, and no means of control, *Vermontborg* drifted onto the Capelle reef near Lihou on 3 January. She drove so far up the reef on the 9.2m high tide that it was uncertain whether there would ever be enough water to get her off. If that were the case she would have had to be broken up. Importantly for Guernsey's seashore and wildlife there was no pollution threat, and no danger to life.

Klyne Marine Salvage were given the contract, together with Smit Salvage. They surveyed the ship and identified that a tide with potential for refloating would occur on 5 January, but that it would be the last possible tide for some time.

For the public, the sheer size amazed onlookers. The carparks at Perelle and L'Eree were full, and people abandoned cars all along the coast road. *Vermontborg* rested on an even keel, and at low tide it was possible to walk right around her. She was a ship out of scale with all around it - people looked like insects next to her giant propellers.

VERMONTBORG

The Receiver of Wreck warned that the tradition of looting wrecks was wrong, though it was pointed out that there was nothing on board. The police put up 'do not cross' tape to deter the public from approaching the ship, but this was widely ignored and the tape was trampled into the sand.

A 12th century chapel, the Dom Hue, once stood on the same reef so the States Museum Service cordoned off the site to protect the remains from being damaged by crowds. *Vermontborg* was a huge draw, with thousands wanting to see a bit of maritime history. Numerous pictures were shared on the internet.

Helicopters took pumps and generators to the ship, and the water ballast was pumped out. A security team was called in for public safety, and scaffolding was put up around the wreck. Two tugs prepared for a salvage attempt. The 'Prosperity' car park at Lihou was closed to cars for use by helicopters. The first attempt, on a 7.7m tide, failed as the ship was too heavy and the tow bridle snapped. More patching and lightening of

the hull was done, but another attempt on 17 January also failed when the tow rope snapped.

Meantime, Guernsey's surfers took advantage of the new attraction. Capelle reef is a good surf break, but the presence of *Vermontborg* made it even better for those who chose to surf right alongside this massive hull.

The best tide so far was 8.7m on 18 January, and it proved slightly higher with the swell. Just 13 minutes before the high at 6.51pm *Vermontborg* slipped off the reef in rough seas and driving rain. The salvage master Henk Smith led the operation as the tugs took the strain. The vessel moved, then stuck, moved again, and finally after 30 minutes she moved out to a safer position. Local pilots guided the tugs through the rocks to deeper water.

By 2004 *Vermontborg* had been fitted out and sold to a German company and renamed *Winona*.

W. J. Caparne

AVERTING DISASTER

THE LIGHTHOUSES

THE HANOIS LIGHTHOUSE

c. 1932

LOCATION

Built on the most westerly point in the Channel Islands, the Hanois reef.

LIHOU ISLAND

HANOIS LIGHTHOUSE

HANOIS REEF

Well into the nineteenth century, the absence of a lighthouse on the west coast of Guernsey resulted in regular shipwrecks on a coast that saw a very significant amount of shipping but had no navigational aids.

The most westerly point in the Channel Islands, the Hanois reef, had always been dangerous for shipping. It is a bearing point, a turning point, and the first landfall from the west. Even during the controversies raging in 1840-60 over the building of a lighthouse, there were several more wrecks. Two more wrecks between 1860-62 as the lighthouse was under construction increased the urgency.

Cornish granite was considered to have the best qualities for a sea-rock tower, and this was sourced at the Carsew quarries near Penryn in Cornwall. The preliminary planning decisions had taken much time, choosing exactly which rock in the reef to build on, making visits, taking measurements, and estimating costs. When the rough granite from Cornwall arrived in St Peter Port it was laid out on the Castle breakwater for dressing and numbering. Later it was carried by barge along the south coast to the Hanois reef.

Le Bisseau was the rock chosen as the site and, because building proper foundations would have been difficult, the base of the tower was constructed around a protruding stub of rock for extra strength. The elegant tower had a 'waisted' design, being about 9m diameter at the base, 5m at the waist, and 6m at the top. The light, made up of 672 pieces of glass, would be over 30m above high water.

The 2500 tons of granite blocks were dovetailed for strength in a novel way,

vertically and horizontally, which became the standard model for the iconic towers of the south-west such as Eddystone and Bishop Rock. Not even storm waves could dislodge blocks when huge waves crashed against the tower and sent spray right over the lantern. When building the Fastnet lighthouse in Ireland, the same design and the same Cornish granite were used.

The Hanois lighthouse is widely considered to be one of the finest lighthouses in the British Isles.

A helicopter platform was constructed on top of the tower in 1979, making the regular relief of keepers easier and more reliable. Solar panels were added when Trinity House automated the lighthouse in 1996. It was the end of an era when the last lighthouse keeper, Robbie Goldsmith, was taken ashore and the integrity of the light was left to the computer skills of a monitoring officer.

THE CASQUETS LIGHTHOUSE

LOCATION

Built on the Casquets reef,
5 miles west of Alderney.

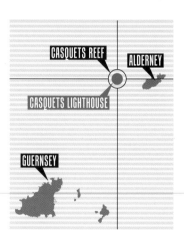

The steep-sided Casquets reef stands in deep water as a natural obstacle between England and Guernsey, and it has taken a heavy toll on shipping. This great line of rocks lies 5 miles west of Alderney and is surrounded by treacherous currents and dangerous overfalls. Nearby, the Alderney Race and the Swinge are the two fastest currents in the English Channel. The hazardous rocky outcrops of Ortac and Burhou are between Alderney and the Casquets.

In the early 1700s there was discussion about the need for some sort of light on the Casquets. In 1701 the merchantman *Michael*, on passage from London to Lisbon, was wrecked here and nine of her 16 crew managed to clamber onto the rocks. They ate limpets at first, but after a week and no rescue they ate their dog. Finally after 17 days they were saved by a passing ship.

In 1723 Thomas Le Cocq, proprietor of the Casquets, obtained a patent from Trinity

S. L. Kilpack

THE CASQUETS LIGHTHOUSE

Captain J. S. Cates, 1837

House to build a light of particular character to distinguish it from those on the English and French coasts. Three 6-metre towers were built, named St Peter, St Thomas and Dungeon. Each had a coal fire inside a glazed lantern, and they were first lit on 30 October 1724. The dues collected were one half-penny on English vessels and double for foreigners. The lights were upgraded to oil-burning in 1779.

It is recorded that when lighthouse engineer Robert Stevenson visited the Casquets in 1818 he was not impressed, describing the lights as "unsatisfactory and most rudely got up".

The family of Louis Hougre ran the lighthouse for much of the early 1800s, but in 1849 three keepers were appointed working a roster of two at a time on the rock. A large bell was also installed as a fog signal. Between 1853 and 1855 substantial alterations were made to the Casquets: the towers were raised to increase the range of the light, and larger lanterns were fitted at a cost of £4,748.

In 1877 the lights were reduced to one on the St Peter tower, with a character of three flashes every 30 seconds. The other two towers were reduced in height and a fog siren was installed in the Dungeon. A diaphone was added in 1922, a radio beacon in 1928, and in 1939 a radio telephone was installed.

With the fall of France in 1940, the Casquets was shut down and the keepers taken off. The Germans soon occupied the station and fortified it with barbed wire and anti-aircraft guns. On the night of 2/3 September 1942, a British commando raid named Operation Dryad was launched against the Casquets. The 12-man

Rev. John Hall, c.1793

team caught the German soldiers completely unaware, and they were taken back to England as prisoners. During the raid the commandos destroyed the German radio equipment and picked up some code books.

During the period 1950-54 new electrically-powered machinery was installed and the present character of five flashes every 30 seconds was established. In 1990 the Casquets light was automated.

SELECT BIBLIOGRAPHY AND FURTHER READING

Adams, J. **Medieval Wrecks in St Peter Port Harbour, Guernsey.** University of Southampton, 1998

Adams, J. & Black, J. **From Rescue to Research: Medieval Ship Finds in St Peter Port, Guernsey.** Centre for Maritime Archaeology, Southampton, 2004

Couling, D. **Wrecked on the Channel Islands.** London, 1982

Dafter, R. **Guernsey Wrecks: Wrecks around Guernsey, Alderney and Sark.** Tonbridge, 2001

Dafter, R. **Guernsey Sentinel: The Remarkable Les Hanois Lighthouse.** Tonbridge, 2003

Masterton, S. **A Century of Shipping in the Channel Islands.** Guernsey, 1985

Monaghan, J. **The Story of Guernsey.** Guernsey, 2010

Monaghan, J. **Guernsey's Gallo-Roman Ship and Evidence for Maritime Trade.** Guernsey, 1993

Ovenden, J. and Shayer, D. **Shipwrecks of the Channel Islands.** Guernsey, 2002

Ovenden, J. and Shayer, D. **The Wreck of the Stella: Titanic of the Channel Islands.** Guernsey, 1999

Pickford, N. **The Atlas of Shipwreck and Treasure.** London, 1994

Rule, M. & Monaghan, J. **A Gallo-Roman Trading Vessel from Guernsey.** Guernsey, 1993

Sarre, J. W. **Guernsey Sailing Ships 1786-1936.** Guernsey, 2007

Sharp, E.W. **Lighthouses of the Channel Islands.** Guernsey, 1979

Woodman, R. and Wilson, J. **The Lighthouses of Trinity House.** Bradford on Avon, 2002

Transactions of La Société Guernesiaise, in particular:

David, J.M. **Wrecks in the Bailiwick of Guernsey.** Vol. XVII, 1961

Sharp, E.W. **Wrecks in the Bailiwick of Guernsey.** Vol. XVIII, 1967

Historic Newspaper reports and unpublished sources (Priaulx Library)

The Guernsey Evening Press

The Guernsey Magazine, 1872-79

The Guernsey Weekend Press

The Star

The Quarterly Review of the Guernsey Society, 1952

The Weather diaries of Elisha Dobree (1777-1846)

ACKNOWLEDGEMENTS

Kit Hughes and Matt Harvey of Guernsey Museum assisted with the research, archival data and provision of illustrations. Additional information and archival data came from Martin Crozier of Guernsey Met Office, Sue Laker at the Priaulx Library, Pat Thompson of the Guernsey Press, Colin Le Conte of Digimap Ltd, Granite Le Pelley, the UK Hydrographic Office, Buz White MBE and Richard Keen for which the author is grateful. Book design by Paul Le Tissier.

We are grateful to everyone who has given permission to use the photographs, illustrations and paintings used in this book.

Every effort has been made to check ownership rights of the images used in this publication. Please contact us if any acknowledgement has been omitted or incorrectly attributed and we will amend future editions.

www.museums.gov.gg